© 2017 Michael Adam Gaut
The Painting Poet™
All Rights Reserved

*Dedicated to the memory of a
dearly beloved friend,
father, husband and more—
Ryan James Casullo,
who worked jubilantly with Buffalo youth,
placing musical instruments
in their hands—
and art in their hearts.*

This collection is comprised of twenty-three poems, written and repeatedly revised between 2008-present; many have been plucked from the depths of the subconscious, and the tale they tell is open to interpretation...

going in circles

between alpha and omega—
maybe—there is some force from within
which keeps everything moving uniformly,
some kind of spin, controlling motives
uniformly—best as it can
but what do I know, i'm no compass;
i'm merely armed with a pen

the torch or the curse

when my story
like those before before me
is retold, rewritten,
reversed—
my soul will explode
of the tongues of young poets,
passing the torch or the curse

small plate

i thought about quitting
and knitting my wit's end
but someone said poems
make for great friends
my first, middle, last kiss
good morning, goodnight
breakfast, lunch and dinner
a snack at late night;
i eat this to survive
i drink this and imbibe
sustenance for the mind

slam

if only i could
read your mind
hoping in this open
book i'd find
your contour map
thoughts inclined
designer form
frame of mind
past rains,
cloudy eyes
dew mornings
rainbow skies

with silver wings
you don't tread light
sterling angels
stunning sights
sing your songs
wrong or right
off pitch, off key
or just off night
i will not judge
you in that light

after the waiting

after all the midsummer sunsets
after all the harvest moons
after the frigidity of sad winter
after the feigned return of some spring
after all which appears golden, or green
after all the bullshit fairy tales
after all the conquered civilizations
after all the broken hammers
which attempt to build and rebuild
and build and rebuild upon tattered,
two-dimensional reflections
of our trampled, bleeding hearts…

the honeybee to a mate

i am but a black and gold blur
and a putrid sound to most
but for a moment's buzz
when i have you in my sights
i put you in my song

you're one in a billion
in a field of just millions
and i just want a taste
of your sweet photosynthesis

box of love

could you put your love inside
could you do it, if you tried?
could you put your love inside?

i'll give you just an empty box
with a bottom and a top, and
four walls to darken when it closes
but we can't see, so we don't know it

you won't know, if you don't try
can you put your love inside?
can you, will you?

can you and will you be surprised?
if you can put your love inside...

breathe

at the time of writing this poem
i had lived for 11, 271 days
taking, roughly, 21,000 breaths per day
for a total of 236,691,000 breaths
and while that might seem
like a large number
it puts a number
on how many i have left
and makes me wonder
what i'd do, if i somehow knew
that i had only one last breath—

i would draw it from my lungs
as a lead pencil kiss
shared like a no.2 secret
between paper lips
& let your story fill
my baby blue parallels

in Brandon's name

i woke up to an alarming number
of texts and phone calls,
emails and Facebook Notifications—
during the night, a friend was shot and killed—
the season's freshest quilt
conspired to cover green earth that day
but nothing could purify the frigid, greedy truth
nothing could say it wasn't so
a young man, only twenty turns at a year
his smile so bright it might only
be measured in light;
my heart pains for his family's darkness
my head aims at understanding
if swords are built to defend
then for what purpose are those shields?

his walk had a mellow, smooth pace
his voice was calm, not known to race
cracking his shy exterior
wasn't as complex as it might seem
he was keen to music and lyrics
he was smart and he was humble
he had open ears to hear you
when offering advice
on the kind of things only time can tell
and now I am reminded again of the things
history cannot prepare the human heart to tolerate.

f®ameworthy

my unstable frame of mind is a weary sovereign state
my sorrowed state of place is a scary sober nation
where six figured contraband elevates inflation
elemental combinations form the promise of the land
manmade reprise for all that had been taken
and all shall be forsaken in the swallow of the sand

depths below the surface, feeling atmospheric worthless
i've asked myself the purpose, and
been nurtured by her hands—
skinned by kin and herded with all who had been blurred
between the lines which had been written
and delivered to the band
a black sheep living riddled with the difficult decision
if love is to be given—or precisely other hand
when backed into an ocean, helplessly floating
one can only hope for an honest piece of sand

childhood

back when everyone was young
and we had grandpa's land
what a different time that was
everyone smoked and nobody cared
the world seemed larger and
there was little in my way
besides a poor sense of direction
i wonder how i ever found my way
out of those desolate woods

ode to the trees we slaughter

thank you for the air i breathe
and then chop, thank you for heat
thank you for homes and for furniture
thank you for aspirin (i think)
thank you for paper and for poetry
thank you for life and for death

staring at your open autopsy
i count your blank expression
reading between concentric lines
i find time for suggestion
knowing many of your suitors
nearly drowned you in their ink
i forget my lover's quarrel
and return you to your sleep

your move

hunger screaming from grass rooftops
insects strung up and named suicidal
or called flag; there is no humanity
or eight legged teardrop
brass faucets ripping window dressed stereotypes
down the drain with leftover bicycle standards
raping wannabe-innocent, hillbilly lawyers and
butt-fucking the great blue
whatever
i am what i am if not what i'm able,
they say,
retribution for nationalistic statistical draft overflow
i suppose sadness glows in the televised moonlight—
cramping a never ending rain of devastation
ugly enough to eclipse Saturn, then turn, turn
to return.
forever left surrounds her
a corn kernel from self-indulgence
and galactic fields from Cessna stripes
and atomic football snowflakes
i am what i am if not what i'm able

where's the yellow sub station?
who is the red handed bully?
who has seen the green eyed goblin in charge?
give away something for nothing
i dare you

comic relief

time, i've heard them say
is but a messenger for death
a reminder
that we are little more
than a remainder of our breath
life is hollow as the quill
feeding flight to the feather
and empty as promises
promised forever
as our looming
impending doom spells disaster
we arrange words
to standup and form laughter
and call me depressed, but
whatever comes after
must be a sight for sore eyes
considering factors
like Earth pollution
oppressive institutions, and
no solution for cancer

so as a joke—
i propose a toast—
to the tall dark man
in the long black coat

if this ship's going down
let's rock the boat
one last time before we go

pretend tonight is our last
and turn spirits up high
put fear in the past
for tomorrow we die

who says we are the perfect distance from the sun?

i walk outside to find my face frost bitten
or my entire body overheats
where i live, the changing seasons
might mean today: summer solstice
and tomorrow: shovel snowdrifts
we are made of metal
but we rust; we decompose
disintegrate, putrefy, dust
sift below ground and return
as an island equidistant to love
and bad decisions;
i am three minutes from soul
shadowed eternity
i am Alaskan night and sad blue day
yellow-stone rich i am
and i will split this rock
into a billion big bluffs
and recollect her essence in a song

candy store

i love to go grocery shopping
it is a guilty pleasure of mine
it makes me feel like a fat kid
in a candy store
i suppose that's because i am
quite literally
a fat kid—in a candy store
only this candy store is packing
so much more than candy
you ever notice how our grocery
stores have so much more than groceries?
it ain't just bread and milk at "wal-mart," folks
you can get your flu shot there
your prescription glasses
snow tires!
all just a few aisles apart
fill up your cart with a dozen eggs
two-dozen roses
a DVD about Moses
and three ceramic yard gnomes
you found in the 'home and garden'
section, right next to the hoses you might find
a pound of frozen butter
pick up a birthday card for your mother
buy some chocolates for your lover
or maybe you need a new microwave
or you've saved for an Xbox one or PlayStation 4
or maybe you never got passed that PlayStation 3
maybe you just came to see what you see, and
buy on the fly—a real impulse spender!
maybe you want to become
the world's biggest collectible coin vendor
so you are shopping through price guides
which say what they're worth

maybe your wife like's your sex life just fine
but you've convinced yourself she wants more girth
by secretly peeking into those magazines
discussing opinions and notions
on that eternal topic of size versus motion
maybe you need lotion for your psoriasis
a four-slot toaster, a whole chicken off the roaster
a set of glass coasters, or a Bob Marley poster
the point is that we take all this for granted
and the more i think about it—i really can't stand it
there are people living and dying in streets of sand
and i can't even imagine driving them to a "Sam's"
and explaining to them that
about once a month, or even once a week
i might come here to get everything I need
anything i need or desire i can find it right here
from lawn chairs to beer
so i throw a fit when they don't have my brand of chips
and they stopped carrying my favorite 'hot pocket'
and they only have six flavors of dip
and they moved the cigarettes, and they've gone past
ten dollars a pack! and can you believe our shopping cart
kept creaking and squeaking like that?
"i really have it bad," an American might say
to an indigenous friend
who would look back in amazement, and say,
"have you gone off the deep end? Do you have any idea
what people in the old village would do if they had this?"
they'd probably die from eating a Twinkie
(not before having some god-awful shits)
but fuck it! we got Pepto-Bismol right here on the shelf!
and some anti-reflux medicine to manage
your acidic health—
in fact, with so many health products;
so much medicine and food—
our grocery stores, especially these mega supercenters—

would probably look more like a sanctuary
to someone we so rudely describe as hailing
from a "third-world nation"
perhaps someone truly poor—
but with all of my American audacity
i see it as *a fucking candy store.*
and that is sad—truly sad—it just isn't proper
even my pen and my pad came from a "price chopper"
now i can easily call myself a poet, but
what should i write, that hasn't already been
advertised on a gradient green case of sprite?
my words aren't grrrrrrrrrrrrreeeeeatttt!!!!!!!!
they don't go snap, crackle or pop—
they just go round in circles until i'm back at the top
a "tops" supermarket, that is—
i'm here, again, shopping for stanzas
there's truth in these aisles
if you push through propaganda

lost and found

give me a piece of your mind
allow me to keep it and share it—
give me a piece of your heart—
i will nurture and care for it
give me a piece of your soul
and i'll remember to bear the names
of each piece of the puzzle
who made me more aware of it
helped me to see that we are, indeed
part of a puzzle—or a chess game—
where there is bad in the easy
and good in the struggle
and the lavish distractions
of the hustle and bustle
has me asking more questions
as if i need more feathers to ruffle
what is it all worth in a nutshell?
is it the obligation of the philosopher-poet
to prophesize and reflect
with a ponderous pen and nostalgic notebook?
or is it enough to entertain, like a metaphorical clown
impregnating minds with rhyme
like "baby, this is ultrasound,"
i can take you to new heights, where new types of
sophisticated clouds surround the ground
and we go leaping mental bounds
through mesmerizing rhyming and pitch perfect timing
i'm Cy Young on the mound, or Mike Tyson fightin' rounds
the real deal, the ear biter surprising crowds
and knocking out the proud with my style—so profound
but so it don't go over heads
i've always kept it underground
and if you leave something with me—
I will be your lost and found

war never ends in a tie

war never ends in a tie.
although, coincidentally, most modern wars
start with men who wear them.

nobody ever gets "even,"
never reach that impossible equilibrium
if one military confirms "x" number of kills,
must the other seek to eclipse them?
why do world-leaders not aim at worldwide,
unconditional, amicable, mutual compromise?
and why can't war just end in a tie?

a grudge is not a healthy thing to hold on to
grudges never end in a tie
if you hold disdain against your enemies
does it go away once you've done them wrong?
i do not think so. A grudge never ends in a tie
how many times can we "get each other back?"
how many times can we "taste our own medicine?"
vengeance is a poisonous sin. revenge never ends in a tie

lives are expendable.
positioning is key
war never ends in a tie
families mourn
division enhanced
war never ends in a tie
choose a side, fight or die
war never ends in a tie
war never ends in a tie.
war never ends in a tie

everyone loses in war, war does not end in a tie
humanity forever scarred, war cannot end in a tie

when bridges have all been burnt
war will not end in a tie
war will not end in a tie
war will not end in a tie

dominant prey on the herd
the world does not end in a tie
disease no longer cured
the world cannot end in a tie
poets, they mutter their words
the world will not end in a tie
the world will not end in a tie
the world will not end in a tie
fife is not fair, the poets declare
and war does not end in a tie

dear mirror

i was young and i lied to you
and only you know all the times that i've tried to
repent
but i only repeat
all my crimes—
from the inside out
i've been turned on a dime
for a dollar
and i've dealt with the devil
i fear i'll be suspended in Hell
from now til forever;
no matter how clever, sharp or impressive
i keep digging my way
to deeper transgressions—
a reflection of my relentless, foolish indiscretion
the deal i accepted acknowledged this seven-year sentence

it's not breaking the mirror
that brings the bad luck
its breaking trust with the image
with whom you have to face up

do you even love poem?

i was asked during a live performance
if i would read a love poem
but, my love poems have all been buried, said i
scribed on the walls of ancient pyramids and then
poof! vanished in the sands of time!
even if discovered—the Da Vinci coded, hieroglyphic design
is much too deep to decipher; too divine to define

but this particular audience member persisted
"please, you must have *one* love poem"

i do not. i mean, i did, but
they've each been folded neatly
then placed in an envelope
and sealed with a kiss, and sent off
on the first cloud i saw
that looked like a spaceship

so i would love to help you, you see,
but i'm afraid you wouldn't understand my love poems
because they are out of this world.

eternal

until my body lie silently in a casket in church
until six men carry me from the backseat of a hearse
even when my soul roams in a place beyond earth
my spirit will reside in the soul of my verse

when six feet of dirt has been
displaced to make space for me
and i'm placed beneath ground
in a wood case that was made for me
even when my soul stays
in some place beyond earth
my spirit will reside in the soul of my verse

poetry, an ocean

dear mother poetry,
an ocean of thankfulness
would not be grateful enough
for letting us utter your name
i pray to you, and i pray for the lonely
who sail you; captaining the courage
to awaken you—
only to be lost in your vast tidal waves

mother poetry,
an ocean of thankfulness
would not be grateful enough
for letting us utter your name

daughter

if i ever have a daughter
she will punch rainbow holes
through cardboard skies
and wear clouds to school on mondays

when other kids point and laugh, and ask,

"what is it?

she will point and say,

"none ya damn nimbus!"

my daughter will know the difference
between two thousand, one hundred and fourteen
And five hundred and seventy six:
it's one thousand, five hundred and thirty eight—
which doesn't really matter
but i would like for her to be good at math
simply because math is hard
and she will be good at lots of things
but other things won't come so easy
and i'm eager to see how many obstacles she overcomes
when she's beaten-down by the pressures and stressors
which seem to take our breath away
i'll make sure to be right there
filling her lungs with the hope and the knowledge
that while tomorrow may be no guarantee,
it does come with the promise that
yesterday is a page that can be reread, revisited—
or ripped up and forgotten

if i ever have a daughter
i would like for her to see the world

to feel the coastline between her toes
to taste the sea-salt lingering in the air
i want her to fall—in love
if love is what drives her
i want her to learn if learning inspires her
i want her to know no one can confine her
to any set role or ever attempt to define the word "her"

i will teach her that our conscience is prison
if and when you have committed the crime, or
the mind is a garden where innocence thrives
i'll tell my baby she'll sleep well at night
if her true beauty resides in a knowledge of self-worth
which is devoid of pride, but overflowing with all
which we've deemed dignified

if i ever have a daughter
i can't wait to hear what her mother names her
though, i fear that the sound of her name, alone,
will draw arrows sharper than Sirens Songs
aimed at Cupid's pleasure—and perhaps
I will feel like a wounded soldier does
when the day comes for my daughter to marry
and I am left to carry a piece of that epic struggle
while acknowledging she is someone else's fight now

if i ever have a daughter
i want her mother to know, right now,
that i will be faithful until i die
and that all these words i write down
will forever be dedicated
to the love she has shown me
so—if ever the day comes—
she simply outgrows me
i promise to do right by our daughter
because i want her to know me

as a man of my word
in a world full of phonies;
salespeople, sideways crooks
and sidewinders, heck,
i'm not so stupid, as to think *my* daughter
won't start a few fires—
pull some alarms
ring someone's bell
get kicked out of school,
put someone through Hell
she might do all the things
her mother and i beg her *not* to do
and we will still love her
the same way i hope your parents love you

if I ever have a daughter
i will arm her with compassion and wit
she will punch rainbow holes
through cardboard skies
and wear clouds to school on mondays
when other kids point and laugh, and ask,
"what is it?"

she will smile and say,

"today it's nimbus—
sorry if my choice makes me seem delirious,
tomorrow, tuesday, i will be more cirrus"

if ever I have a daughter
she will punch rainbow holes
through cardboard skies
and wear clouds to school on mondays

Made in the USA
San Bernardino, CA
16 May 2017